ABOVE: *A forest of bottle ovens and pall of smoke adjacent to housing characterised each of the six town centres of the Potteries. This photograph of Century Street, Hanley, was taken in about 1905.*

COVER: *'Blue Bell Works, Longton' by Reginald Haggar, AI*

THE POTTER

David Sekers

Shire Publications Ltd

CONTENTS

Set in 10 on 9 point Times roman and printed in Great Britain by C. I. Thomas & Sons (Haverfordwest) Ltd, Press Buildings, Merlins Bridge, Haverfordwest.

ACKNOWLEDGEMENTS

The author thanks the Gladstone Pottery Museum and the many people who have contributed to its photographic collection for their generous help. They have provided most of the illustrations in this book. Specific sources are as follows: Blakes of Longton, page 8 (top); British Ceramic Research Association, pages 8 (bottom), 10, 29 (top); Frederick Calvert, *Picturesque Views of Cities, Towns, Castles, Mansions . . . in Staffordshire*, 1830, page 3; City of Stoke-on-Trent Museum and Art Gallery, cover, page 1; A. J. Cope, page 7; Robert Copeland, pages 20 (bottom), 23, 29 (bottom); *Cup and Saucer Land*, 1908, by courtesy of Rev J. Graham, pages 25 (bottom), 28, 31 (both); Gladstone Pottery Museum, pages 22 (bottom), 30; Phil Hewitt, page 13; *Illustrated London News*, pages 19, 24; H. and R. Johnson-Richards, pages 11, 15; Knight, *The Land We Live In*, 1845, pages 5, 25 (top left); Medical Institute, Hartshill, pages 22 (top), 25 (top right); *Pictorial Gallery of Arts*, c 1845, pages 18 (bottom), 21; *Rees Cyclopaedia*, 1815-19, page 14; Shaws of Wolstanton, page 6; D. Shelley, page 27 (top); *A Representation of the Manufacturing of Earthenware*, 1827, pages 16 (bottom), 18 (top), 20 (top), 21; Mr Stanham, pages 16 (bottom), 27 (bottom); Twyfords Ltd, page 12; J. Wedgwood & Sons Ltd, page 9.

The potbank yard, c 1845.

The rural surroundings and pitted hilly countryside of the Potteries is captured in this illustration of Tunstall dating from 1830.

EARLY DEVELOPMENT

The story of the Staffordshire Potteries has rarely been told, and yet this area of the Midlands has a far richer character and a more distinctive heritage than many better known parts of Britain. Here a skilled and industrious workforce, located in an isolated rural backwater and, often in wretched conditions working with the simplest of tools and raw materials, made objects of great beauty and worth and won a worldwide reputation for themselves and their native area. The many unpleasant facts of life in the Potteries, which were common even in recent memory, have been obscured by the scores of books on the wares produced, but the character of the Potteries was formed by the 'potbanks' and the working life and people they enclosed.

The early country potters, throughout Britain, worked on a small scale, often supplying only local markets, near the sites where they found their clay. They faced competition first from the metropolitan centres, such as London, Bristol or Norwich, where from the sixteenth and seventeenth centuries British and foreign craftsmen captured important high quality markets, and then from a rural, isolated and otherwise undistinguished area of England, North Staffordshire.

During the seventeenth century the community of potters working around Burslem began to use coal as a fuel and this appears to have given them an economic advantage over other rural workshops still dependent on diminishing supplies of timber. Coal was abundantly available, outcropping on the crests of ridges throughout the area now known as the Staffordshire Potteries. The slender supply of ivory clay was soon consumed, but the red or blue firing Etruria Marl still occurs in abundance. From the late medieval period Burslem potters are known to have supplied Midland markets with simple cylindrical butter pots and other domestic wares, and their competitive prices, noted as far afield as Nottingham, indicated that remoteness from the large metropolitan markets would not be a disadvantage for very much longer. As Josiah Wedgwood noted, by 1710 Burslem had become a prominent pottery centre, probably the largest in Great Britain, and had acquired a name for skill and craftsmanship.

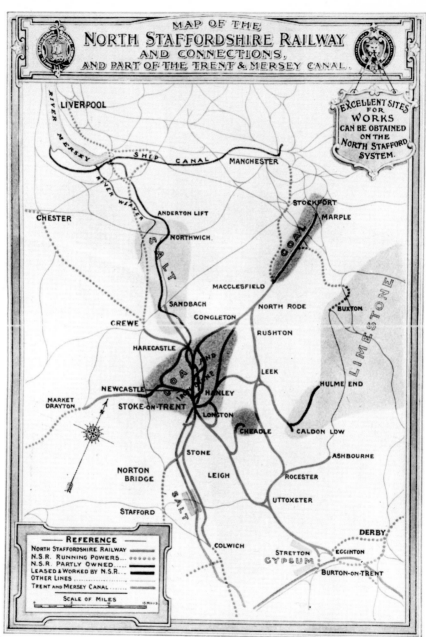

The geographical assets of the area surrounding the Staffordshire Potteries are illustrated on this map from a 1921 handbook on North Staffordshire. Red clays were abundant in the vicinity of Hanley and Newcastle, while fireclays were associated with the coal measures. A complex web of railway and canal routes had transformed an isolated and rural area into an industrial centre.

The Trent and Mersey Canal winding its way to Longport, from a print of 1845. The bottle ovens of Burslem, the 'mother town' of the Potteries, dominate the brow of the hill and pollute it with their smoke. The nearby countryside, however, remains unspoilt.

THE GROWTH OF THE SIX TOWNS

The Potteries may look like one long sprawling conurbation, with little to distinguish one town centre from another, but the core of Burslem still survives, as do those of Tunstall, Hanley, Stoke-upon-Trent, Longton and, to a lesser extent, Fenton, the town which Arnold Bennett forgot when he referred to 'the Five Towns'. These towns had their rivalries, dialects and special characteristics, and each was surrounded by smaller satellite village communities which were gradually engulfed as the towns grew. In 1910 the Six Towns were unwillingly united to form one city called Stoke-on-Trent. The older borough of Newcastle-under-Lyme, a mile or so to the west, retained its independence.

Tunstall is the northernmost of the towns. It stands on a ridge surrounded by old tilemaking and brickmaking sites, some of which probably date back to the late middle ages. Decorative ceramic tiles are still made in Tunstall by H. and R. Johnson-Richards Tiles Ltd, but the town is also known as the home of the Adams dynasty of potters, as well as Alfred Meakin, Booths, and Enoch Wedgwood.

Burslem town centre still has the street plan of a small medieval market town. Earthenware is the town's speciality and pottery factories still cluster around the civic buildings and shops and sprawl out along the main roads. Some of the grandeur of Burslem in its heyday can be discerned in the Georgian facade of Wood's Fountain Place Works, the portico of the Sunday school and the fine frontage of the house built by Thomas and John Wedgwood. Obadiah Sherrat, John Walton and other figure makers worked in Burslem. The poorest workshops stood by the wall of St Paul's churchyard, which still has an unkempt and dismal air. After 1777, when the Trent and Mersey Canal

Fresh Air from the Potteries.

Atmospheric pollution grew during the nineteenth century as the output from the factories expanded. Intermittent clouds of smoke became dense and unremitting, blotting out the sun. This postcard appealed to the self-deprecatory humour of local people, but won Stoke an image which it has had to fight hard to shrug off. Behind the smoke the skyline of Longton may be discerned.

was opened, groups of factories and houses were built near to it. Only a few outbuildings of Davenport's works at Longport still survive, but the works of Dunn Bennett, Burgess and Leigh, and Arthur Wood and Son still stand along the canal bank. Of the Burslem which Arnold Bennett described with the thinnest possible disguise, only a few buildings remain. These include the Wedgwood Institute and Library of 1869, the Town Hall (the most imposing building in the Potteries) and the Leopard public house.

Hanley dominates the next hill on the road south and was an important mining town surrounded by colliery spoil tips, but these have been reshaped and landscaped. Hanley is the shopping centre for the Potteries, but the few bottle ovens still surrounding the heart of the town prevent it from being as featureless as many other modern shopping centres. One bottle oven belongs to Dudsons, another to J. H. Weatherby and a third to a brushmaking company. Masons Ironstone ware is still made in a handsome early nineteenth-century factory not far from the town centre. On the site of the old Bell pottery stands the new City Museum and Art

Gallery, which houses one of the finest and most extensive collections of historic North Staffordshire wares. Nothing is left of the sites of other memorable Hanley companies, like New Hall, Neale & Wilson, Mayer, Meigh, or Brown-Westhead and Moore.

To the north of Hanley is the ill defined area of Cobridge, where from the 1750s colours for enamellers were manufactured, and where a number of decorating studios were located. To the west lies Etruria, where all that is left of the Wedgwood works is the Round House built on the southern end of its famous facade; the factory was demolished in the 1950s, the village for Wedgwood's workers twenty years later. Etruria Hall, however, survives. To the south-west is the suburb of Shelton, near the Caldon Canal, where the workshops of John Baddeley and, later, the Ridgway factory stood.

Stoke-upon-Trent had always dominated the other towns by virtue of its ecclesiastical supremacy, as the controlling parish of the area. Its valley setting gave it the early advantage of canal transport and later the main railway station to serve the area. The most famous names associated

6

with Stoke-on-Trent are still thriving firms — Minton and Spode. Biltons and the Portmeirion Pottery have adopted Stoke, but of the old Goss works only the bottle ovens now remain, and the Minton Hollins Works, which have a splendid long tile-decorated frontage, stand empty.

Fenton is shorn of landmarks. Fenton's greatest son was Thomas Whieldon, the pivotal figure in the history of the Potteries in the eighteenth century. The site of his works has been excavated but nothing remains of his house. Among other distinguished Fenton potters were Miles Mason and his son Charles, and the firm of F. and R. Pratt, whose mid nineteenth-century colour printed earthenwares were highly successful.

Longton was known as Lane End and, colloquially, as 'Neck End'. Until the last decade of the eighteenth century it was remarkable only for its coal mines and ironworks but from the nineteenth century it developed into a major centre for the production of bone china. Of the older firms like Turner or Hilditch, only one, Aynsleys, survives, but many china firms still dominate the town, such as Paragon, Royal Albert and Royal Adderley Floral. One typical old china factory now houses the Gladstone Pottery Museum.

A clear aerial view of a Potteries town centre could only be obtained during holiday weeks when none of the factories were firing. This view of Longton shows dozens of bottle ovens crowded together in the town centre, where along with shops, terraced houses and pubs they had sprung up in a completely un-planned manner. Living and working conditions in this town remained poor until after the Second World War, when the worst areas were bulldozed.

ABOVE: *Red firing clay, or marl, for common earthenware, was the commonest and most easily accessible of the Staffordshire potters' raw materials. It was dug out virtually on the doorstep of the potbank, as can be seen in this photograph of a marl pit taken in Longton in 1905. The plateway in the centre of the picture conveyed clay into the heart of the factory. Disused parts of the pit were filled in with the potters' debris, known as 'shraff'.*

BELOW: *The proportion of bone in a bone china body is almost fifty per cent, so quantities of animal bones were imported to the Potteries to be calcined and ground like flint. This pile of calcined bones was photographed before milling.*

Flint was an essential ingredient for white firing earthenwares and stonewares. Flint pebbles were brought from the east coast via the river Trent, then prepared by calcining (that is burning to make them friable) and then grinding to a powder in pans immersed in water, as shown here. This photograph was taken at Wedgwood's own flint mill at Etruria about 1900. Independent flint millers usually supplied potters with dried flint in dust form, and it is still an essential ingredient for the industry.

TYPES OF WARE

CERAMIC BODIES

Earthenware was the fabric first produced by the North Staffordshire potters. The local red clay, sorted and purified but unmixed with other ingredients, then fired at a fairly low temperature (950-1050 C, 1742-1922 F), remains somewhat porous. When fired to a higher temperature it becomes much harder and more impermeable and, in this state, provides the material for red, brindled and blue quarry tiles as well as engineering bricks.

China clay from Cornwall, ball clay from Devon, flint from the east coast and, later, Cornish stone were all imported into the potteries by the 1740s, in an effort to find satisfactory ingredients for a truly fine white body to emulate that of imported wares. The fine white earthenware evolved

by Whieldon and then Wedgwood (known as creamware) is based on these ingredients. The term 'pottery' is often used loosely to signify earthenware.

Stonewares are like earthenware but are fired to a higher temperature and are vitrified and thus non-porous and stronger. Traditional stonewares, common in Europe since the middle ages, were grey or buff coloured. A bright white stoneware body, suitable for salt glazing, was perfected in North Staffordshire by 1730. The salt-glazed stoneware of the eighteenth century should be distinguished from the early nineteenth-century Staffordshire ironstone wares of firms like Ridgway, Mason and Spode. Their stoneware, stone china and ironstone china were adaptations of earthenware bodies, significantly strengthened and made more opaque.

Porcelain is a term only loosely associated with the Staffordshire Potteries. Of the three types of porcellanous ware the Potteries can claim to have perfected only bone china and made it their own.

Soft-paste porcelain's ingredients resemble those of glass; early potters assumed that the glass-like appearance of oriental porcelain was reproduceable with such a formula. In Europe, and in the eighteenth century to a lesser extent in London and other British centres, some fine soft-paste porcelain was made. Great losses on firing were common and the ware was suitable for decorative items rather than tableware. The Longton Hall factory was one of the few Staffordshire firms to experiment with it.

Hard-paste porcelain did contain two of the ingredients used by the Chinese. Known as kaolin and petuntse, they were found in England in china clay and Cornish stone. Few British firms other than Plymouth, Bristol and New Hall in Hanley succeeded in making hard-paste porcelain.

Bone china's recipe was similar to that of hard-paste porcelain, but with an addition of fifty per cent animal bone ash. This formula resulted in wares which were easily modelled, resembled fine translucent oriental wares, withstood thermal shock, were equally suitable for useful as well as decorative wares and were not too costly or difficult to fire.

CERAMIC WARES

The potters of Staffordshire have always made pottery as a commercial undertaking, without local patronage or subsidy. The earliest items produced were butter pots and other domestic wares such as storage jars, salt kits and cooking pots. Useful earthenwares have been made ever since and following the development of Wedgwood's creamware the tablewares of

Fine china produced in Britain has been admired throughout the world and continues to be produced in hundreds of patterns to the very highest standards by firms like Spode, Royal Worcester, Coalport and Minton. A selection of Royal Worcester's post-war range is seen in this photograph.

The production line of a tile factory c 1910. As the girl on the far left is demonstrating, the tiles were produced by whirling the fly press. The young assistants stacked the fragile tiles in saggars ready for biscuit firing.

the Potteries earned and retain a world-wide reputation.

At the same time potters were aware of the demand for decorative and ornamental wares. They rarely tried to compete with the finest products. Wedgwood's first ranges of jasper and agate are exceptional in this respect: the earthenware figures of Neale or Wood are more typical of the Potteries. The popular market for chimney ornaments and 'toys' was also richly served by many anonymous makers of portrait busts of newsworthy figures, fairground scenes, animals of all sorts and the familiar cottages which were often designed as pastille burners. Statuary porcelain, known as Parian ware, became popular in early Victorian England. It was derived from the eighteenth-century continental 'biscuit' figures but firms like Minton and Spode succeeded in producing such figures to a high standard in large quantities.

This was the first of many eclectic phases in which the Potteries evolved rich varieties of decorative effect and embellishment derived originally from continental techniques. Among the finest examples are Minton's *pâte-sur-pâte* vases, colour-glazed majolica designed as fountains and bouquets of china flowers to decorate figures and vases. Although some of these skills are now less frequently used, the traditions of useful and ornamental wares still flourish side by side in the Potteries.

The clay beds in the area of Tunstall were used before the seventeenth century for making tiles and bricks. This industry, which remains widely dispersed throughout Britain, continues in its traditional and modern forms in the Potteries: some firms still have the old clay pits, beehive kilns (the last type to give up firing coal) and open-air stacks of special blue bricks, finials and quarry tiles. The brickmaking industry is, however, being rationalised throughout Britain. Modern plant now exists side by side with the old at

Fireclay baths must have been among the heaviest objects to have been fired in bottle ovens. Having been press-moulded, here they are being fettled prior to biscuit firing at Twyfords, c 1905. Twyfords were at this time also one of the largest manufacturers of lavatories.

Longport and Silverdale and already many old sites of tile workings have been obliterated.

Decorative glazed tiles were made in the same parts of the Potteries and sprang from a similar tradition. Medieval encaustic tiles were probably also made locally, decorated with designs inlaid with pale coloured slip. The technique was revived there, at Worcester and in the tile works on the river Severn in the 1830s and 1840s. The church and state were prominent early customers; then a general market was developed and geometrical inlaid floor tiles were provided for homes throughout Britain. Meanwhile faultless white dust-pressed tiles were being produced in quantity for the first time and, unlike earlier tiles, they proved suitable for walls; bathrooms, public houses, hospitals and food shops were decorated in a material that suited the demands of the first generations of the hygiene-conscious. By the beginning of the twentieth century, a separate market had developed for ready-made tile fireplaces. Other pottery centres, such as Poole, Derbyshire and Doultons of Lambeth, provided the architectural faience and terracotta which adorned many high street buildings erected between 1880 and 1910, but the Potteries acquired and have retained the lead in the manufacture of decorative ceramic tiles.

The revolution in domestic sanitary requirements after 1880 provided the market for Twyfords, Armitage and others to supply sanitary ware — lavatories, baths and wash-basins — combining engineering skills with ceramic experience. One of the most modern manufacturing units of its type in the world has recently been built in the Potteries.

The same hard-paste porcelain fabric which is suitable for oven-to-table ware and faultless white tableware is also a resilient electrical insulating material. Since about 1900, when the electrical industry was in its infancy, ceramic insulation has taken over a large part of the market from glass, resin and other experimental materials. Large insulators are still often hand-thrown and turned, assembled and glazed, while small components are usually dust-pressed.

The clay measures found adjacent to coal seams often have excellent heat-resistant properties. These refractory clays were probably used for making bricks for kilns at an early date and also provided the essential ingredient for the bodies of *saggars*, the containers which hold pots in the kiln. In the twentieth century the use of refractory clays for kiln furniture, refractory bricks and crucibles has grown.

A non-recyclable by-product of all potbanks was shraff. This was made up of broken or imperfect wares rejected at various stages of the manufacturing process and has for many years formed the waste tips and even the hard core of the Potteries' landscape. This close-up view of a sight characteristic of the Potteries landscape was taken at Middleport tip, showing Wolstanton colliery in the background.

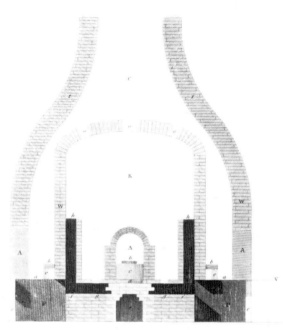

Horizontal Section

This plan and section of a bottle oven dating from 1815 shows a structure well developed to assist and control even firing. It changed little subsequently. The vertical section shows an inner structure (the oven) enclosed by an outer funnel-shaped shell (the hovel). A doorway to the hovel permitted the fireman access to the four firemouths. Another door in the oven enabled the ware to be placed inside, usually in containers called saggars. The horizontal section shows the interlocking system of flues, which distributed the heat from the firemouths into the centre and sides of the oven.

14

Calcining kilns were sometimes given the shape of bottle ovens. This group of ten was used for burning raw materials before they were crushed and mixed into the body for tiles. Like bottle ovens, their profile was rounded and fitted with metal 'bonts', and the stacks were ornamented with denticulation.

BUILDINGS OF THE POTTERIES

Traditional potbanks were built with bricks and roofed with tiles although towards the north and east of the Potteries brick gives way to limestone. Roofing tiles made locally replaced thatch from the eighteenth century. The shape of potbanks seems to have evolved from the shape of rural houses and barns, the house often facing the road, the barns frequently enclosing a yard at the back.

The cone- or bottle-shaped ovens were the striking feature of early potbanks. They were not peculiar to the Potteries, having evolved in successive stages from the medieval and post-medieval kilns in which the pots were placed separate from the heat

LEFT: *By the early years of the nineteenth century the yards of many potbanks had developed into busy drying, packing and dispatch areas. The ware boards, panniers, baskets, crates, barrow, cart, dray and tubs in this print of 1827 illustrate all the available modes for transporting the fragile product.*

BELOW: *Little had changed by the beginning of the twentieth century, when this photograph was taken. The hazel and willow crates were peculiar to the Potteries, providing the most reliable containers for packing china and earthenware.*

from the surrounding fire boxes. By the end of the seventeenth century it is thought that this type of kiln was occasionally surrounded by a hovel, a separate structure acting as a chimney to control and direct the draught upwards, which presented the characteristic bottle outline. Throughout the eighteenth and nineteenth centuries the size of hovels increased as did the amount of smoke they produced, thus provoking complaints from the end of the eighteenth century. Ceramic tiles, sanitary ware and

electrical porcelain were similarly fired, while bricks and quarry tiles were fired in down-draught *beehive* kilns of a squat profile, familiar throughout Britain.

In the early twentieth century a number of down-draught bottle ovens were built, in an effort to increase the efficiency of the firing process, and they would have had a chimney stack alongside. The smaller kilns, rarely over 30 feet (9 m) high, which may sometimes still be seen in the Potteries, were *muffle* kilns used for the final, or enamel, firing. Oven builders seem to have dictated the final shape of their ovens and varied the denticulated brickwork round the stack as a minor decorative feature. The iron bands, or *bonts,* which were a characteristic feature of many ovens, had a stabilising function: they expanded as the oven warmed up and contracted as it cooled. So strong was the tradition of oven building that many calcining kilns, which worked quite differently, were built in a bottle shape, and even a windmill, a mile south of Longton, is built with bonts.

The bottle ovens were the life of the potbanks. They originally dominated the yards, but later, in the nineteenth century, they were often enclosed by buildings so that only the top portion of the stacks emerged from the workshop roof. The workshops, characterised by stark func-tional simplicity, outside staircases and simple brick window arches, became larger during the nineteenth century. Mining subsidence (which was prevalent throughout the Potteries), dilapidation, cramped sites and the absence of any rational planning gave many potbank yards a haphazard and disorganised appearance.

Facades, on the other hand, were often models of neat architectural design. The pediment, bell tower and classical frontage of Wedgwood's 1769 Etruria works set a style that was often imitated in the Potteries during the succeeding century. The main roads, and parts of the Trent and Mersey canal embankment, were lined with impressive and orderly rows of orthodox classical buildings, each intersected by an archway leading into the yard, with the manager's office above. The most eccentric variant on this pattern was Enoch Wood's Hilltop Works at Burslem, where an elaborate castellated gateway and Gothick cottage were grafted on to a Palladian facade.

The distinctive features of these buildings were little recorded before the development of new tunnel kilns broke up the traditional pattern. Modern factory buildings reveal nothing of the processes which occur within, and while the outlines of Stoke-on-Trent are rapidly becoming neater the area is losing its character.

Enoch Wood's Hilltop Works at Burslem had the most eccentric facade in the Potteries. Most other potbanks emulated the classic simplicity of Wedgwood's Eruria works. Here the plateway provided for horse-drawn coal drays. It winds round under the bell tower and through the archway into the pot-bank yard.

ABOVE: *Until the mid nineteenth century clay preparation was an arduous manual operation. After the tanks of slip had been stirred by a paddle (just visible in the background), the water is boiled off, 'leaving a clay about the consistence of dough', according to the caption to the original print.*
BELOW: *Sliphouse work was rationalised by organising the layout so that the slip suspension moved by gravity from process to process. Here, in the early Victorian period, it is poured through sieves to purify it.*

The tank on the left is known as the blunger, and the frame sketched on the right is part of a filter press. Cakes of dewatered clay are being taken from the filter press and rolled up, before being taken to the clay-making departments.

MANUFACTURING PROCESSES

Traditional expertise seems to be the main reason for the continuation of the pottery industry in North Staffordshire long after the local clays had become unimportant and the ready access to coal had become unnecessary.

PRODUCTION

Each company usually had its own recipe. The clays were mixed in water in a tank, at first with paddles, then from the last third of the nineteenth century in mechanical *blungers*. The mixture, called slip, is strained through sieves to remove grit and other impurities, and traces of iron are removed by magnets. The water has then to be eliminated, traditionally by natural evaporation: the slip was poured into a large sun-pan and left to dry (one such sun-pan still exists at Wetheriggs Country Pottery, near Penrith in Cumbria). The dewatering process was probably accelerated at an early date in the Staffordshire Potteries by placing hot flues un-der the slip tank; an engraving of 1827 shows this method. The mechanical innovation which transformed this essential preliminary process was the filter press. Needham and Kite's 1856 patent was for a press to separate yeast from beer, but it was readily adaptable for use in the manufacture of pottery, and by the end of the nineteenth century it was in widespread use. The filter press, which is still seen in potteries, pumps the slip into woven envelopes which are squeezed together to force out the water, leaving cakes of hard and relatively dry clay, which are then removed from the press.

The clay is next prepared for shaping. If plastic clay is required it must be kneaded to remove air bubbles and give it uniform plasticity. Kneading or wedging was a laborious and even injurious occupation. The development of pugmills in brickfields by the 1820s established the principles of mechanical kneading but they were applied only slowly and intermittently in pottery

19

ABOVE: *The thrower could use both hands to control and shape plastic clay into pots using a kick-wheel. His output would be greatly increased when he could engage to help him a 'baller-up', to weigh out balls of clay, and a person to turn the rope-driven flywheel. This illustration of 1827 shows this manufacturing unit, which had become an established feature of production in the Potteries by 1750.*

LEFT: *The thrower used a gauge to help ensure that a succession of pots had identical proportions, and he also used ribs or 'spoons' made of wood, slate or earthenware to provide the correct profile and finish. In this photograph of c 1900, a selection of ribs hangs on a nail on the wall by the thrower's shoulder.*

manufacture, where it is doubtful that pugmills were widely used before 1900.

When the potter required slip, the suspension of clay in water had to be clean, and, for efficient production, of a specific clay content or pint weight. So the dewatered clay was weighed and again mixed in a blunger with a measured volume of water. For tiles, electrical porcelain and for small items which could be best pressed into shape (like teapot lids), the clay had to be dried further and then ground into powder.

Plastic clay is required for throwing on the wheel and has traditionally been necessary for making tiles, bricks and saggars and for pressing. Moulding shapes in plastic clay developed into a widespread craft in the Staffordshire Potteries. Before the end of the eighteenth century moulds were commonly made from biscuit-fired clay. The *flatware presser* used a *batter* to flatten the plastic clay into a *bat,* which was then draped and pressed on to moulds for dishes. At a few factories oval dishes are still made by hand in this traditional way. If a foottrim was required it had to be added by hand. The *holloware presser* made figures, teapot spouts and cup handles right up to the 1970s. Figure making required some dexterity and, even before plaster of Paris moulds were used, Staffordshire potters seem to have produced small and attractive pressed figures and groups in large quantities.

Plastic clay was difficult to control in mechanical production. Machines for making holloware and flatware, known as *jollies* and *jiggers* respectively, were introduced only slowly into the Potteries after 1830, partly because the potters opposed them and partly because of their mechanical imperfections. The machines work on the principle of shaping the plastic clay with a profile tool pivoted on an arm, simulating the hand of the thrower as the clay revolves. Jiggers normally formed the shapes of the reverse side of flatwares and jollies the shapes of the inside of hollowares. At first plates made on the jigger tended to develop cracked backs during firing, but such problems were overcome towards the end of the nineteenth century and nowadays all domestic flatware and most domestic holloware is produced with highly automated plant, using plastic clay.

Slip is thought to have been used in the manufacture of some of the fine stonewares attributed to Elers in the 1690s. The suspension of clay in water adhered to the inside of the porous biscuit mould, which

Plastic clay, after batting out into a uniform sheet, was draped over or pressed into moulds, a skill known as flatware or holloware pressing.

21

ABOVE: *Holloware making machines were developed in the 1840s and introduced quite widely, but only after much resistance, a generation later. It is not known why they were called 'jollies'. The profile tool forming the inside shape of the holloware item (while the outside was shaped by a plaster of Paris mould) was controlled by the potter but required much less skill or effort than throwing.*

LEFT: *The machine which formed the profile of the reverse side of flatware is still known as a 'jigger'. In this photograph of c 1920, the profile tools can be seen hanging from the joist. The young mould-runner had to supply his master continuously with fresh empty moulds and take the filled moulds to the drying stove (seen in the background). The sufferings and punishments of the young mould-runners in the nineteenth century were recorded by C. Shaw in 'When I Was a Child'.*

The shapes of all pressed and cast figures and wares were first produced by the modeller. The skill of the modellers for Parian ware was unsurpassed. This Spode modeller of c 1900 had to ensure that the numerous separately cast parts of each figure could be stuck together seamlessly.

slowly absorbed the water until a shaped skin of drying clay could be removed. Until about 1770 this process was far slower than holloware pressing. Then plaster of Paris began to be widely used for moulds as it readily absorbed water from the slip and thus accelerated the slip-casting process. In the early twentieth century it was found that the proportion of clay in a slip could be significantly increased by adding deflocculants. Far less water then needed to be absorbed and slip could dry in moulds in a matter of hours, rather than days. As a consequence, slip-casting became the most common method of producing holloware and the skills of the holloware presser became obsolete.

The use of clay in powder form is comparatively recent. By the mid nineteenth century several industries in the Midlands had perfected the technique of pressing powders into marketable shapes (for confectionery or buttons, for example), which was adopted in the Potteries, using a *flypress*, for the manufacture of tiles. Powdered clay, of a uniform moisture content, gave tilemakers fewer drying, warping

and firing problems than plastic clay. Today powdered clay is used in the manufacture of tiles, bricks, saggars and components for electrical porcelain.

After being shaped by throwing, pressing or casting, the clay (or green) wares may need to be trimmed or *fettled*, while fine hollowares may need to be turned, and limbs, heads and bodies, from separate moulds, had to be assembled into figures. No machine can replace the trained hand or eye of the potter at this stage. Even drying is essential for all green wares. Potters traditionally prefer to dry pots in the open air, but from the early nineteenth century special stoves or hot cupboards were common features in the manufacturing units. Since the 1920s the cupboards have been replaced by trays revolving in drying chambers.

Decorating before the initial biscuit firing is no longer widespread. The best known type of clayware decoration is *sprigging*, the application of ornament in clay form from miniature moulds. Incised decoration, common in many pottery areas, has been less common in Staf-

23

fordshire. In the seventeenth century *sliptrailed* wares were frequently of a very high standard, but this tradition died out at the end of the eighteenth century. A medieval decorating technique using slip was revived in the middle of the nineteenth century in the manufacture of encaustic tiles, for which the pattern was poured on to the clay tile in a sequence of coloured slips. This was a conscious attempt to revive a medieval craft and did not endure beyond the First World War.

BISCUIT FIRING

Many wares needed to be fired once only. Bricks, pipes, quarry tiles, salt-glazed stoneware, saggars and statuary porcelain, which required neither decoration nor glaze, needed only a single firing. In the seventeenth and early eighteenth centuries lead glaze was applied to the green ware in dust form, providing some examples of once fired lead-glazed ware. For other types of ware the biscuit firing was the first of successive firings. Nowhere was the traditional skill of the potter more essential for the success of the manufacturing company than in firing.

Wares were placed in *saggars*, containers made of refractory clay. Flatwares were carefully bedded in flint to prevent warping and china figures were propped up with stilts to prevent sagging. The saggars were placed in the oven under the direction of the *cod placer*. The pattern of setting in the saggars conformed to the established pattern on each oven and varied from oven to oven and potbank to potbank. Generally speaking, the outer rings of saggars needed to contain wares that could withstand the most intense heat; the bottom of the oven would also contain a larger volume of ware per saggar, to absorb and conduct the heat from the firemouths, while the tops of the stacks or *bungs* usually were filled up with empty 'green' saggars, which themselves needed to be biscuit-fired before they were fit for use. The fireman would take charge of the placed oven, organise the *lumping* (the initial filling of the firemouths), the kindling and the gradual build-up of heat. He was able to control the very primitive oven by regulating the dampers built in the crown of the oven and adjusting the regulating holes set in the sides of the oven

Placing wares in saggars required special knowledge. Plates were 'reared' or 'dottled', that is carefully separated from each other by thimbles, as illustrated here, to prevent the glaze from making them fuse together in the glost firing.

above the firemouths. Many a fireman reckoned to bring an oven up to temperature (1000-1150°C, 1832-2102°F, for earthenware) by experience and eye alone. The colour of the flames would provide a guide to temperature and the porosity of trial pieces drawn from the oven during firing — detected by letting the piece cool, spitting on it and seeing how fast the piece absorbed the spittle — would indicate how the firing was progressing. Rule of thumb was never entirely replaced, and by far the greatest risk of financial loss on a potbank occurred during firing: firing losses of twenty to thirty per cent were not uncommon in the days of bottle ovens. Temperature measurement devices, such as pyrometers, Bullers rings, Holdcroft bars

ABOVE LEFT: *The scene inside the hovel, where placers are bringing saggars full of ware to be stacked in the oven. This arduous procedure remained unchanged from the eighteenth century until bottle ovens were replaced by tunnel kilns. An oven might contain two thousand saggars, each weighing up to half a hundredweight.*

ABOVE RIGHT: *Inside the oven the saggars were placed in 'bungs' some 16 feet (4.9 m) high, in concentric circles so as to fill the oven. The ladders used by the oven men were known as 'osses' and were removed before firing commenced.*

RIGHT: *The man in charge of firing, the most critical operation in the whole cycle of pottery production, was the fireman. Many a factory manager or proprietor stood in awe of his fireman, who was by far the highest paid employee. The whole output of the factory was placed in his charge and a bad firing could produce catastrophic losses. After kindling the firemouths, the fireman had to stay up with each oven, often for 72 hours on end — a job which gave firemen a proverbial thirst. An average-sized biscuit oven could consume in that period 10 or 12 tons of coal. The fireman had to control each firemouth and judge when to increase ventilation or temperature and when to leave well alone. How much beer an average fireman consumed is not recorded.*

and Seger cones, provided increasingly reliable guides to oven firemen, but losses were only significantly brought under control when tunnel kilns were developed.

The Staffordshire Potteries, with a few exceptions, were slow to replace bottle ovens with tunnel kilns, where the wares were placed on trucks, pulled through a long tunnel lined with refractory bricks, through zones of increasing temperature, until they emerged, fired, at the far end of the tunnel. The process was continuous, dispensed with saggars and eliminated the loss of time in placing, waiting for the oven to cool and drawing. One factor constraining firms from investing in this new technology was lack of space. Another was a disinclination to invest at a time when capital investment on a large scale was almost unheard of in the Potteries. The pre-war move of Josiah Wedgwood and Sons to a purpose-built factory at Barlaston, five miles to the south of Etruria, heralded a twentieth-century industrial revolution in the Potteries and tunnel kilns were widely adopted by the other larger firms after the Second World War.

After firing, biscuit ware is quickly checked and graded, brushed to remove dust from the firing and stored before being taken on to the next process.

UNDERGLAZE DECORATION

The objective of the potters who applied decoration before glazing and glost firing was that the decoration should be permanent and sealed under the glaze. Another consideration was the use of cobalt blue, for centuries the most fashionable and desirable decorative colour, which would develop only at a high temperature, so it could only be applied before the high temperature glost firing. Any subsequent firings would have to be at a lower temperature.

Between about 1750 and 1830 much underglaze blue decoration was applied by hand, but simultaneously the transfer printing process was gaining ground. Once the image had been engraved on a copper plate, it could be continually reproduced without further artistic intervention. By 1830, many firms were using engravers working in independent studios, while the more important companies, like Spode, employed their own. The engraved copper plates were warmed on a stove, coated with the prepared colour and then wiped clean, leaving the incised image containing the enamel colour. A sheet of prepared tissue was laid on the copper plate and both were fed through a simple roller press by the printer, to transfer the image to the tissue. Then the cutter would cut out the separate parts of the pattern. The senior transferrer would apply each piece of tissue to the ware, then the second transferrer would rub, brush and press it on to transfer the image to the ware. When immersed in water, the tissue paper would float off. This slow and meticulous process was accelerated when certain firms installed rotary copper plate printing machines in the second half of the nineteenth century, which produced long streams of transfer-printed paper. Since the 1960s, transfer printing has been further automated by the development of the Murray Curvex machine, which transmits the engraved image, robot-like, to the ware through a mechanically controlled ball of gelatine. Biscuit ware which has been transfer-printed usually requires a low temperature 'hardening on' firing before glazing.

GLAZING

Tinglaze was hardly ever used until the ceramic sanitary ware industry grew up at the end of the nineteenth century. The most common glaze ingredient was raw lead, which, until the middle of the eighteenth century, was commonly dusted on to green ware. Thereafter it was more scientifically adapted to suit the new ceramic bodies, to withstand thermal shock and to enhance the appearance of wares. It was then applied as a liquid in suspension, for many decades by brushing, then by dipping, and nowadays often automatically by spraying. Staffordshire potters of the late eighteenth century and early nineteenth century were masters of the art of applying glazes stained by oxides as a form of decoration for plates and then figures — a technique revived in the mid nineteenth century by the manufacturers of majolica. Leadless glazes were sought from the mid nineteenth century, to mitigate the injurious effects of lead on the health of dippers, and have been adopted universally in the Potteries in the last fifty years.

ABOVE: *This photograph was taken in a transfer printer's shop in the 1930s. The circular plate on which pigment is warmed, to soften it, is known as the 'backstun'. The printer on the right is applying the pigment to one copper plate, while the man on the left is carefully detaching the engraved tissue from another after it has passed through the roller press.*
BELOW: *The dipper was a highly skilled employee, who carefully immersed each item of ware in the vat of glaze, shaking off any surplus. In the days before fritted lead glazes, lead poisoning was virtually inevitable among the dippers.*

On-glaze enamel decoration is here being applied to typical Staffordshire chimney ornaments. It is interesting to note that these typical Victorian wares were still popular at the turn of the century when this photograph was taken.

GLOST FIRING

Wares dipped in glaze had to be handled with care as they were again placed in saggars. To prevent them sticking to each other during this firing process, they were separated by items of *kiln furniture* such as *stilts, spurs* and *thimbles*. The manufacture of such items was undertaken on each potbank, until, at the end of the nineteenth century, firms like Bullers specialised in their supply. The saggars were placed above each other, on wads of clay, to seal them from the sulphurous fumes at the start of the firing which could otherwise discolour the glaze. In other respects the firing for glost would follow the pattern of biscuit firing, taking from twenty-four to thirty-six hours to reach peak temperature and half that time to cool. The oven would be similar, but as glazes volatilise during firing, adhering to the walls of the saggars and of the oven, glost saggars and glost ovens were used specifically for glost firing.

The drawing of glost ware from the oven was a careful process. Whereas the biscuit saggars were often upturned and the biscuit wares heaped in baskets, glost wares were handled with more care and struck against

each other to detect imperfections (a resonant ringing sound was expected of perfect ware).

ON-GLAZE DECORATION

Underglaze decorated wares often required no further manufacturing process; they would be sorted, checked and stored ready for dispatch. But a wide range of on-glaze decoration was traditionally applied at this stage. Enamel colours, made of metallic oxides, were developed in the Cobridge area from the middle of the eighteenth century. Nowadays, firms supplying enamels to the industry are often subsidiaries of extensive conglomerates.

Until recently most colours available to the decorating departments needed to be fired on at a lower temperature than the glost firing, and accordingly an enamel firing (or successive enamel firings) at temperatures of 500-800°C (932-1472°F) was required to fix the on-glaze decoration.

The skill of hand painting has been on the decline since the first decades of the nineteenth century: the pressures of industrial production helped introduce less time-consuming decorative techniques such

28

LEFT: *The subtle mottled colour ground on fine wares from the eighteenth century onwards was achieved by dusting on the raw pigment. Blank or reserved areas of plates were varnished and surplus pigment was removed, latterly by using a dust extractor, as seen here in the background, since the raw metal oxides are poisonous.*

BELOW: *Placing a muffle kiln. The greatest care was necessary at this stage of the manufacturing process, as each item had by then acquired a relatively high manufacturing cost. This photograph shows fine Spode wares in the early years of the twentieth century.*

as 'tint-on-print' (colouring in parts of transfer prints) and multicolour on-glaze lithographic transfers. Amongst specialised decorating skills, *bat printing*, which was a method of applying a very delicate on-glaze stipple engraving effect, was common at the end of the eighteenth century. *Ground laying* or colour dusting was a continental method of applying a richly coloured ground to glost tableware, kept in production by the better factories until the 1960s. Finally, the art of the gilder, which has been developed since the early years of the nineteenth century, is still the pride of the best china manufacturers in the district.

ENAMEL FIRING

This was traditionally carried out in an enamel or muffle kiln, distinguished from the bottle oven by its smaller size and its single chamber, surrounded by flues, which separated the wares from the flames. No saggars were, therefore, necessary: the wares were carefully placed on bats and equally carefully removed after the short firing cycle. Some of the early experiments in continuous firing kilns were for enamel firing, but today it is more common for gas-fired intermittent kilns to be used.

29

Youngsters were employed to do menial and routine tasks in potbanks within living memory. None was more menial than the job of batting out the bottom section of a saggar. Two of these seven boys photographed in 1921 were saggar makers' 'bottom knockers'.

CHANGES IN WORKING CONDITIONS

Many of the pictures in this book relate more vividly than words the conditions in which North Staffordshire potters worked for so long. As in many industrial centres, the first stage of the industrial revolution did not result in a deterioration in working conditions. A partly rural craft-based skill, such as pottery making, only became an injurious occupation as industrialisation progressed, bringing into the overcrowded town centres poor workers from the countryside. In the early nineteenth century, when many young firms were struggling to survive, the larger firms were following the example set by Wedgwood at Etruria in recruiting and organising the labour force and separating departments and skills.

In 1842 the state of the industry was revealed in the report of Samuel Scriven, the Government Commissioner, on 'The Employment of Children in Factories'. It revealed the harsh lives of the 'mouldrunners' and the 'wedgers', the long hours, bleak discomforts, extremes of temperature, miserable diet and fierce punishments inflicted on the young workforce. It also drew attention to the prevalence of industrial disease in the Potteries. For the next hundred years this was a burning issue. Mortality rates in the Potteries were indeed high; the main problem was diagnosed at an early date — lead poisoning. Dippers were particularly prone to this. Although experiments with leadless glazes are recorded throughout the century, lead was essential and the safe solution adopted and approved early in the twentieth century was a lead glaze of low solubility, produced by making the glaze suspension out of fritted lead. Controls have had to be imposed on the use of other poisonous metals which brought grave risks to colour manufacturers and to careless enamel decorators, especially ground layers.

The next serious health risk endured by potters was pneumoconiosis: flint dust particles when inhaled caused gradual and often fatal damage to the lungs. It was a lingering disease, which took many decades to diagnose and control. Those most at risk were flint millers, oven men who had to bed china biscuit ware in flint inside the saggars (where silica now replaces flint), slip-house workers and fettlers of biscuit earthenware. Flint is still used as a component in the bodies of many wares, but the risk of pneumoconiosis has been reduced by the Factory Inspectorate, which insists on proper ventilation and cleanliness of workshops and on protective clothing.

In the 1860s, when Dr Baker, the first Factory Inspector in the Potteries, was recommending such controls for the first time, he met with considerable opposition from pottery companies. Public opinion then believed that frequent alterations of excessive heat and cold were more injurious to health. The reform of industrial disease in the pottery industry was largely due to Dr Baker and Dr Arlidge and forms a significant chapter in the history of industrial medicine.

Other vices such as the truck system, excessive drinking, often in alehouses owned and managed by the master potters, and youthful immorality were prevalent and attempts were made to segregate departments of male and female workers.

Many aspects of the rough life of young people in potbanks were recorded in a classic novel of the Potteries, *When I Was a Child* by C. Shaw, which inspired sections of Arnold Bennett's *Clayhanger* trilogy.

It is likely that many small master potters could not afford improved buildings, sanitary arrangements, welfare, ventilation or supervision for their workers. Competition was tough, price cutting common and trade often lean. Until well into the nineteenth century a 'butty' system of employment was prevalent, whereby the journeyman potter hired, paid and controlled his young team of helpers, many of them often children under ten years old.

Disaffection erupted into strikes in the 1820s and 1830s. The jolly posed a threat to employment and provoked an abortive emigration movement in the next decade. Later in the nineteenth century, as the employers grouped together to promote their trade and protect the interests of their industry as a whole, so did the many trade unions. Their descendants, the Ceramic and Allied Trades Union and the British Ceramic Manufacturers' Federation, now have a distinguished record of industrial partnership.

BELOW LEFT: Already by 1900 glass cabinets and extractor fans were being installed to reduce the danger of workers swallowing or inhaling flint dust or raw metal oxides, which were still sometimes brushed on to the ware, as illustrated here through the glass of an extractor cabinet.
BELOW RIGHT: This unusual photograph of about 1900 shows a girl 'wedging', that is lifting and throwing down large balls of clay to knead them into a uniform consistency. Such heavy work injured the chest and heart. In the nineteenth century women and girls working in the brickfields did jobs as heavy as those of the men, but in the Potteries women were usually given the lighter work.

STRUCTURAL CHANGES

Capital investment in buildings and manufacturing plant was not an important consideration for generations of traditional pottery companies. In the post-war period, however, re-equipping became an important issue. The one key item of plant, the tunnel kiln, required substantial capital investment and very often necessitated demolition and rebuilding of large areas of the traditional potbank. The new Wedgwood factory at Barlaston provided an example of the resolution to invest on a large scale. The Staffordshire Potteries have always been intensely competitive, and many firms were stimulated to acquire modern machinery for making cups and plates. The capital structure of the traditional industry was not always well equipped to raise the necessary finance and, partly as a result, new investment required financial restructuring.

The backing of merchant banks and financial institutions played a key role in bringing manufacturers together in groups. Thus, for example, while Royal Doulton acquired and absorbed the firms of Beswicks, Dunn Bennett and Minton, the Allied English Potteries group was formed, combining Booths, Ridgway, Colclough, the Lawley Group of China Retailers, Adderley Floral, Royal Albert, Paragon and Royal Crown Derby. These two groups then were merged under the Royal Doulton name in 1971. Marketing and production have been rationalised, while the brand names have been retained. Investment in new plant, one of the major objectives of rationalisation, has been carried out on an unprecedented scale,

making the Royal Doulton Group one of the strongest international ceramic companies. A similar grouping has been formed under the Wedgwood name. The companies taken over and yet retaining their own brand names in the Wedgwood Group include Adams, Coalport, Midwinter, J. and G. Meakin, Crown Staffordshire and Masons.

Combinations of companies on a large scale have been brought about in the glazed ceramic tile sector (H. and R. Johnson-Richards Group, which absorbed Campbell Tiles, Bootes, Maws, Minton Hollins, Craven Dunnill and several other companies, is now itself part of a larger group), in sanitary ware (Armitage-Shanks) and in insulators (Allied Insulators — Bullers plus Taylor and Tunnicliffe). — smaller groupings include Royal Worcester/Spode, the Alfred Clough Group, Myott and Meakin (owned by the American Interpace Corporation) and Aynsleys, now part of the Waterford Glass Group. One of the lone independents still to survive is Wood and Sons, who trace their origins back to Aaron, Ralph and Enoch Wood, of Burslem.

As such rationalisation progressed throughout the 1970s dozens of ambitious and independent-minded potters decided that, rather than work for a large group, they would set up their own companies. A proportion may yet succeed and prosper, bringing diversity and originality, as well as further investment and employment into the Potteries. From them may yet spring some of the great names and dynasties of the future.

PLACES TO VISIT IN THE POTTERIES

Gladstone Pottery Museum, Uttoxeter Road, Longton, Stoke-on-Trent. Telephone: Stoke-on-Trent (0782) 311378 or 319232.

Minton Museum, Royal Doulton Tableware Ltd, London Road, Stoke-on-Trent.

Spode Museum, Church Street, Stoke-on-Trent. Telephone: Stoke-on-Trent (0782) 46011.

Stoke-on-Trent City Museum and Art Gallery, Broad Street, Hanley, Stoke-on-Trent. Telephone: Stoke-on-Trent (0782) 29611.

Wedgwood Museum, Barlaston, near Stoke-on-Trent. Telephone: Stoke-on-Trent (0782) 4141.